I0483104

The Power of Udemy

An Avenue for Traffic & Massive Exposure

Amy Harrop & Debbie Drum

Disclaimer:

Table of Contents

Introduction

Welcome! We are publishing and content marketing experts, Amy Harrop and Debbie Drum. We help people with publishing and content marketing every single day of our lives and we truly love it!

If you want to learn about us and our work, please visit http://amydebcreations.com/about-us/

Now let's get down to business! There are so many ways to market your content. It would probably be impossible to use every single method because you would be spread too thin—so we need to choose wisely and opt for the most effective ways to get our content in front of a lot of people (with not a lot of work after we create the content). We believe and live by this rule: have the content that you create ONCE work for you over and over again in many different ways. So how exactly do you do this? Well, one of the most powerful ways is to use video.

Video is probably one of THE BEST strategies you can implement today that will change your business for the better. The best part about video is that any written content that is turned into video is now considered completely new content that can be marketed in many different ways on different platforms.

So what do you get when you add video plus a monster marketing platform filled with buyers and tons of traffic every single day? You get massive success!

That platform we are referring to here is called Udemy and every marketer should have a presence on Udemy. We will get into the specifics of what you need exactly to get onto this platform, but we have found that video based online learning courses are a great way to monetize your expertise. Udemy offers a built in audience with hundreds of thousands of visitors a day searching for all kinds of content! It is free to use which is enough of a reason to implement this as an effective traffic source for your content right away.

We are going to share very powerful ways in which you too can grab a piece of this traffic in your niche. One secret that we will share right now with you is that you might already have EVERYTHING you need to literally get started right away creating your course. If you've created content in the past, then you are more than halfway to the finish line! If not, don't worry because it is not hard at all to tap into this treasure trove of traffic and in this book we will show you exactly how to do that.

Let's get into this already so that you can get started immediately with Udemy. One disclaimer before we begin: please keep in mind that, although all of the material in this book is correct to date, it is important that you follow up on any specific rules and regulations from Udemy as it is a third party site that evolves with the marketplace. However, if you follow the basic guidelines, you should be just fine.

Chapter 1: About Udemy

What is Udemy

Based in San Francisco, Udemy is the most popular online learning site. There has been a huge surge in online learning courses now available as the ability to learn and take classes online has grown exponentially. Udemy.com has grown tremendously in the last few years. It is also responding to change. It continually updates its technology and how it promotes its courses, and reimburses its instructors.

While Udemy is not an accredited university site, the classes are offered in a way that is very similar to a university environment. Classes are offered in modular format with individual lectures. Instructors can offer quizzes and also certificates of completion. In addition, there are a huge number of free courses and paid courses available in a wide variety of subjects.

The courses are based on modules where students work their way through small sections of a course and then can review what they have done. Udemy is designed as an e-learning environment where students can learn from their own computer or tablet. It is even possible to download Udemy for the iPad and some other tablets.

As you are going through a course a section at a time and doing things at your own pace, you are encouraged to leave a review at the end of the course.

Why Create a Course on Udemy?

If you are an author, consultant, a service provider, a product creator, or a company that offers consumer goods and services, Udemy can be a great way to brand yourself as an expert and extend your expertise. In addition, you can get paid for teaching and sharing what you know. Having a course or courses on Udemy can help spread the word about additional books, coaching, services, or products you may already have available. Having a course can also build your credibility it can help contribute to gaining a reputation as an expert.

So whether you are still building your brand or your reputation, or you want to reach out to new markets, Udemy can help you with both. In short, there is no reason not to be on Udemy because you can:

- Brand yourself as an expert
- Make money with your course
- Cross-promote your:
  o Books
  o Coaching
  o Speaking events

Overview

The focus of this book is on creating, publishing, and monetizing a video course. You can publish your course in a variety of places. However, we are going to focus on publishing on Udemy. We'll cover:

- Niche and Content Selection
- Creating Your Course
- Uploading and Publishing Your Course
- Monetizing and Promoting Your Course

In order to get the most out of this course, you should take a few moments and really think about what your goals are. Of course that might change as you go through the material, but if you have a clear idea of where you're headed you are going to get much more out of this training.

Set Specific Goals

Before you begin you need to set some goals. Having some objectives identified ahead of time is going to make things easier for you in the long run because you will have a clear idea of where you are headed. Your goals need to be achievable and realistic. Some things to think about include:

- When you want your first course to be completed
- What you want your end result to be

- What you want the result of your first course to be

Think carefully about these goals as they will affect how you spend your time. For example, if you're providing a free course, putting that together is probably not going to be quite as in-depth as a paid course. Most likely you're not going to need to spend quite so much time promoting it either. On the other hand, a paid course will require more time and promotion, but may be more valuable.

Udemy Course Requirements

While we will be addressing many of these requirements more specifically, this is an overview of what every course needs in order to be successfully published.

Course Approval

While you can publish courses at Udemy without getting official course approval, that isn't the way to go. In order to have your course listed in their online catalog, turn up in their search results, and qualify for their promotions, you want to make sure your course is officially approved.

Udemy gets a lot of organic traffic and part of the strategy for publishing a successful course is leveraging that organic traffic.

Here are the official Udemy course requirements:

- http://dna56.com/course

And here are the top ten reasons Udemy won't approve a course:

- http://dna56.com/10reasons

Here is a broad overview of what is required in a course:

- ○ Title & Subtitle
- ○ Course summary
- ○ Course Image
  - ▪ There is an option to have Udemy create it for you (takes about 3 - 4 days)
  - ▪ If you create your own images, the simpler the better
  - ▪ Follow image standards and you can even outsource through a website like Fiverr
- ○ Profile
- A minimum of one hour of content for a course
  - ○ 60% video
  - ○ Written information counts toward content
- Well-organized
  - ○ Introduction
  - ○ Conclusion
  - ○ Sections
- Content Requirements
  - ○ Supplementary material included

- Audio/Visuals clear and meet requirements
- Videos uploaded directly to Udemy

Niche Selection

Some categories are more popular than others. So you can approach creating your courses in one of two ways:

- Choose a niche that is popular and create content around that
- Create a course in an area you are already an expert in

Here are the popular categories on Udemy:

- Business
- Computer programming
- Marketing and promotion
- Online Marketing
- Social Media Marketing
- Creating and distributing content
- Business and Entrepreneur related
- Technology and Computer related
- Entrepreneur
- Arts and Photography
- Digital Photography
- Photo Editing & Manipulation
- Technology
- Health
- Lifestyle

The Expert Approach

If you consider yourself an expert on a topic, for example you've written a book, or if you have an educational background or work experience in that area, then you should see if you can fit your expertise into one of the more popular categories.

If your area of expertise is not in one of the above categories, that doesn't mean you shouldn't publish a course. Just be aware that you may need some additional promotional efforts on your part. You may want to think about how you can rephrase your course in order to target a topic into one of the more popular niches.

Do you have to be an expert?

If you don't consider yourself an expert, you can still publish courses. While you don't have to be an expert, you should have at least a basic understanding of the course topic and consider yourself somewhat proficient.

You can put together your skill set from different areas, especially if you're offering something that's more of a general interest level course, like a free course. You do not need to be a rocket scientist teaching other people how to do rocket science, you can teach information and provide it to them in an engaging fashion. However, you should have a high interest in the topic that you are working with, otherwise the chances of you finishing the project or being excited about the project will really, really diminish.

I know this firsthand (DEB) because it has happened to me. I have been involved in niches that I had no business being involved in and I will never do that again. Even though I know I can put a Udemy course together about anything, I wouldn't just dive into something that I'm not really, really excited about or have the potential to be excited about.

High Interest/Low Competition

You can look at the courses that are popular at Udemy. For example, if you do a course search on Udemy, we can see that a lot of people are interested in how to actually set up and create a blog.

https://www.udemy.com/courses/search/?q=blogging

While there is also an interest in blog design, we can see that there is more interest in general advice on 'how to blog'. Most people who want to get a blog up aren't necessarily interested in learning how to do the technical work like coding and CSS style sheets; they're actually just interested in things like knowing how to get posts up on their WordPress site and making sure things don't break.

BONUS

We've put together some research of low competition/high interest keywords that will help you discover what is already popular, and allow you to do additional research of these topics on Udemy as well.

http://dna56.com/bonus

Research and Keyword Tools

While niche research is a topic in itself, there are some other places you can check the popularity of a niche or topic. For example:

- **Search through Udemy** – you can see price points and how many people have taken classes in specific niches.
- **Google Trends**- http://google.com/trends/
  - A great tool for discovering what is popular, where it is popular, and when it is most popular.

- **Google Adwords Keyword Tool Tracker** – Adwords has become more limited, but you can still get an overall sense of search volume and demand for keywords. You need to have an Adwords account.
- **Clickbank** – Clickbank sells information products. Great place to check what types of information people are willing to pay money for.
- **Amazon** – Another great place for niche research. Check out the best-selling books in a specific niche.

Keywords

When you are doing your research, it's a good idea to start collecting keywords that represent what people are looking for. You can find them in places such as Google trends, book titles and Adwords. Choose the most popular 3-5 keywords for your niche. **You will use these keywords in your course title, description, and marketing**.

Gathering Content for Your Course

Once you've decided what your course topic is, it's time to think about getting your content together for your course. The great thing about Udemy is that you can repurpose content from other areas. So if you have a book or other type of written content you can easily rework the content into a video course.

Udemy does not require exclusive content, so you can get your content from a variety of places. This is one reason Udemy is such a powerful platform.

Free Courses

You can offer both free and paid courses. If you're just starting out, you may want to start with a free course. There are many instances, which we will discuss in more detail later, where you can actually take your free course and leverage that into one of the paid courses. The free course can act as a funnel to attract people, and then you can convert some of those people into your paid course.

Free Course Requirements:

- At least an hour of content
- 60% video

- Can include supplementary and written content toward the hour content requirement

Your free course can act as a production overview of your topic. For example, if your topic is yoga for stress reduction, your course might cover:

- Stress, and how it effects the body
- The benefits of yoga for stress reduction
- Creating a yoga practice stress reduction
- Specific postures that reduce stress

This would be plenty of material and content for a one hour course.

Written Content

The best way to create your course is to start from high-quality written content. You don't need to have a whole book written to actually go ahead and put together an introduction or a free video course on Udemy. You really only need perhaps 25-40 pages or so of written content, maybe even a little bit less.

Where to Get Content

There are a variety of places you can get content. If you are creating a course in your area of expertise you will probably have plenty of articles, training materials, or other types of content which you could convert into a course.

But what if you aren't an expert yet? You'll want to spend some time doing research in your niche or topic. Before you start gathering content for your course, it is highly recommended to create an outline of what you intend to cover. This outline will help you make sure that you have filled in the gaps of what you want your course to include. It will help you make sure that your course is well organized.

Outlining Tips

Here are a few tips for creating an outline:

- **Start with what you know**. Jot down a few of the subtopics you think your course should cover.
- **Start your outline with a mind map**. Mind mapping is a powerful and flexible way to create outlines.
- **Research**. It's good to do a little research ahead of time. Once you've done your own brain dump and have your outline together, you may just want to go and do a little bit more research in order to make sure that you're covering the important points you think need to be covered. It is very easy to get tunnel vision. Try to not get too bogged down in other people's work; just make sure you're hitting the

important things people are going to want to know if they take a basic or introductory course on your topic.

Tip: To create a strong outline, head over to Amazon. Check out the best-selling books in your topic or niche. Use the Amazon look inside feature to preview their table of contents. This is a great starting point for an outline. We really like to look at the *Dummies* ones because they have excellent outlines.

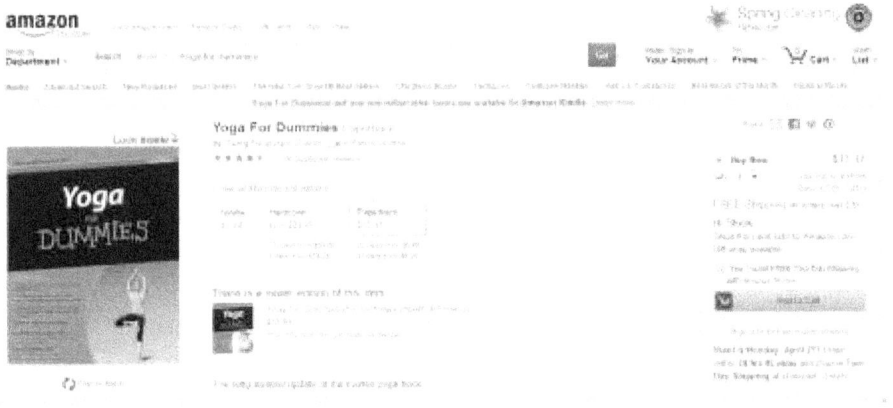

For example, there is a book on Amazon called *Yoga for Dummies*. They don't have a book on 'Stress Relief for Dummies' or 'Yoga for Stress Relief for Dummies' or anything like that, but they do have a book on *Yoga for Dummies*. What's great about this is that they have it broken down into parts and broken down into detailed chapters as well.

To make your outline even better, take a look at the reviews for these books. See what some of the criticisms are about what was left out, and see if you can address those gaps in your course.

You can check out other Udemy courses to get an idea of how to structure your course and also to get inspired or look at things in a different way. Let's say, for example, there is a paid course—*Yoga for Stress;* a $47 course. You may take a look at the course and see that it offers content on breathing exercises, tai chi, standing postures, seating postures, back-bends, and finally there is a green smoothie recipe.

You may look at this and realize that one of the topics that they're not really talking about at all is that a lot of people who practice yoga also have a focus on overall wellbeing and diet. Maybe instead of doing a 'yoga for stress' course, you decide to look into what people who are seriously into yoga like to eat, and how this can reduce stress.

Once you have your course organized and an outline prepared, you can then think about how you are going to create your content. We have developed a special tool that not only will help you create an outline, it will also help you to easily devise your written content and create PowerPoint slides. You can then use these PowerPoint slides to create videos for the majority of your course.

This is an invaluable tool that we developed to help create presentations and videos much faster and easier. You can learn more about this tool here:

http://dna56.com/content1

One type of content that can work very well for part of your course content is what is called 'private label rights content.' This is content that is sold to multiple users, who then change and adapt it to suit their needs. Because you are taking written content and transforming it into video content, the content does not need to be unique to you. However, the content does need to be high-quality, well-researched, and accurate.

We have provided a report of our favorite providers here:

http://amydebcreations.com/contentu

You can also, of course, get someone else to write your content by outsourcing. For a one hour course, you probably only need about 25 pages or so of content. You will then take that content and break it up into smaller chunks.

Here is an overview of where to get content:

- High quality PLR
    - Quality PLR sites
    - Video Courses

- o Written to Video
- o Reports Videos
- Outsourcing Content
  - o Writing with places like iWriter.com or oDesk.com
  - o Videos

Course Organization

The best way to get a feel for how to do your course organization is to go to Udemy and review other courses and see how they are organized. Before you start jumping into actually importing your course content, you should use your outline to organize your course.

Courses are organized in terms of sections and modules. Think of sections as a broad overview inside which you will have specific modules.

Take your outline and organize it into broad sections. For example, if you are doing the yoga course mentioned earlier, you might have three sections:

- Effects of Stress on the body
- How Yoga Reduces Stress
- Specific Yoga Poses

Now you have to figure out what specific modules you will have. Because the course needs to be at least 60% video, if you have six modules, four of them should be video. You can also include supplemental material like PDFs as separate modules. Another option would be to just include them as attachments or additional content as part of your modules. This can easily be done through Udemy.

We will go more into video creation in the next chapter, but your videos should be in the 4-6 minute range. They can run slightly longer if you are doing a demonstration, but shorter is better.

When putting your videos together you need to think about what can you 'show' and what can you 'tell'. Not all of your videos should be information based. You should have some videos demonstrations as well. You should be thinking about what you want to demonstrate and what you would be comfortable demonstrating.

For example, with the yoga course, obvious demonstrations would be someone demonstrating the actual poses. That does not need to be you, of course, you could most certainly use a model. You do not need to have the majority of your course using demonstrational videos, but you should at least have some demonstrations and examples in your course. The amount will depend on your topic.

When you reach the point where your outline is done, you can go ahead and review it. For each section, note 'this could be covered in a video' or 'this would be better as supplementary material'. You can go through and group together your content. This is also a great way of finding out if you have too big of an outline.

Matching your outline with your videos, or your anticipated videos, is going to give you a really good idea of how much material you'll need to be putting together, both in terms of your videos and in terms of your supplemental material.

In addition to your actual course content, which will be delivered in the form of modules, there are a few other things you will want to prepare for your course:

- Udemy requires an introduction and a conclusion for all courses. This could be as simple as a one minute video stating what you're covering or what you covered.

- Be sure to have descriptions for each section and module. If you have these written out in advance, when you're actually uploading your course you can just copy and paste your description into the appropriate area.

Next Steps

 Now that you have your topic selected, your course outline, your course organization and

some content that you can use as the basis for your course, it's time to begin actually creating your videos.

Resources

Here is a consolidated list of resources and information from Chapter 1.

- Udemy Course Requirements:

http://dna56.com/course

- Reasons Udemy won't approve a course:

http://dna56.com/10reasons

- Keyword Research:

http://dna56.com/bonus

- Google Trends: http://www.google.com/trends/
- Google Adwords: https://adwords.google.com/ (Under Tools)
- Clickbank: http://www.clickbank.com/
- Content Transformer: http://dna56.com/content1
- Link To PLR Providers: http://amydebcreations.com/contentu

Chapter 2 - Creating Your Videos and Putting Together Your Course

Moving From Outline to Video

In this chapter, we are going to cover creating your videos and other types of content you can use in your course. Matching your outline with your videos, or what you think you want to have with your videos, is going to give you a really good idea of how much material you'll need to be putting together, both in terms of your videos and in terms of your supplemental material.

Hopefully, you have a folder on your computer where you are keeping all your course materials. You should have your outline document created. You can now open that, save it as a new document, and break your outline down into course sections and modules.

Organizing Your Course

Your outline should now conform to your proposed Udemy course organization. You should have your course organized into several sections, specific modules for each section. Your modules are what will contain your course content.

Your videos should be on the shorter side, as mentioned previously. It's better to have two modules, with shorter videos in the four to eight minute range, than one long module with a 15 minute video.

You can also determine which modules are better served with written material. For example, if you are covering diet in your reducing stress with yoga course, you may want to have one of the modules as a written overview of nutrition requirements and best practices.

Creating Your Videos

Udemy is often fond of saying, "The video is our preferred method of content delivery." Now that you have labeled your course, you should make sure that videos form at least 60% of your course. So, if you have 10 modules, then 6 of them should be video.

Here is some more information about how Udemy calculates your course content length:

- http://dna56.com/calculation

Video Styles

There are a number of video styles available in terms of actually creating your videos.

- **Screencasts** - You can do what are called screencasts, where you're basically seeing somebody's computer screen. These are great for demonstrations, allowing students to 'watch over your shoulder' as you work on the computer.

- **Slideshows** - You can have slideshows, which are basically presentation software slides, such as PowerPoint, with voiceover narration.
- **Combo of both** (most popular) - You can have a combination of both, which would basically be a combination of the slide show with a computer screen, plus demonstrations on your computer. This is really the most popular, and what we will be focusing on in terms of creating your videos. For example, you could be talking about yoga and then show a demonstration on your computer of a website that has a variety of yoga poses.
- **On camera** - You can also have some on camera, as well. It can be incredibly powerful because people get a real-life demonstration of what you are teaching. For example, if you're going to be doing a cooking course, you might want to have some camera demonstrations of you or somebody that you're filming actually putting together the recipe.
- **Mashup** - Udemy also has this thing called a 'mash up' where they let you have a presentation—by default we call it PowerPoint, but it includes any type of slide sharing or slide presentation—and they

let you actually record a video where the video will match up with the slide presentation.

- o This is similar to a college lecture, where you might have the guy standing at the podium and then he has the big screen next to him and he's going through some slides as he's talking. For example, if you're doing a recipe, what you could do is have, on the video section, a video of somebody chopping up vegetables and then on the slide it would say, *A 1/4 cup of celery*, if that's what you were chopping up. Then they would be together on the screen. That would work really well, I think, if you want to demonstrate something but then there's also a little bit of written or technical type of information you want to put in there as well.
- o You can learn more about mashups here: http://dna56.com/mashup

Those are the main types of video courses. We recommend doing a combination of slide sharing and screen capture videos, particularly for your first course. And you can combine these with written material to create your complete course.

Preparing Your Videos

We want to walk you through how you can go from being somebody who is not a video expert or who's new to making videos to actually creating your videos. We're also not talking about spending thousands and thousands of dollars getting videos produced. We're talking about the most time effective ways that you can create the videos for your course.

- Create a slideshow for each video
- Can always edit afterward
- If needed, include specific examples on screen

Scripting Your Videos

Using a script for your videos is a great way to create better videos. We're going to talk a little bit more about editing later, but it certainly helps for editing purposes if you're not all over the place with your thoughts and you at least have an outline.

If you're really good, you can work from an outline, but it can work better if you choose to start with a script. It takes a little bit more effort to make a script, but then, at the end of the day, your videos are going to be much better than you just rambling on or talking off the cuff.

Another thing you can do is create a script for the first few videos that you're doing and then you can check your comfort level and see if you're feeling more comfortable recording your videos from your notes or from your outline.

Then, depending on your comfort level, you may not actually want to have a script for each video because you'll have the information from your outline visible on the PowerPoint slides, but you may feel more comfortable actually printing it out so it's on paper in front of you, or writing out a more specific script.

If you have a second computer, you can actually use one of your computers as a teleprompter. There are some free online teleprompters that will allow you to read the script from your computer. The words will come up and you can be reading them as you're recording your videos.

Teleprompters:

http://www.cueprompter.com/

http://www.easyprompter.com/

Outsourcing Parts of Your Video Production

In terms of outsourcing, you can outsource having your PowerPoint slides actually put together and having the content put on them and you can even outsource getting your notes and your script together, especially if you're getting your content outsourced as well, but it's a good idea for you to be comfortable with the actual making of the videos yourself.

Udemy does really want to see that you're the instructor and you're actually doing the videos. It does make it easier if you've been involved with the content prior to that, but it's not something where you need to have written the content. You could just put it together and then you can be the one actually presenting the videos.

Video Recording

If you want to do it super easy, you can actually record your PowerPoint presentation from inside PowerPoint. You do need a microphone. In PowerPoint, where it says 'Record Slide Show', you can actually record from the beginning. If you select 'Record audio narrations' it'll basically record everything you're doing with the slide show.

So, if you want to get really fancy, if you want to have dissolves and timings and little animations pop up and things like audio narrations, laser gestures and animation timings, you can do that. You can put that into your PowerPoint presentation to make it more dynamic and then you can just stick a microphone into your computer and record your video directly from PowerPoint.

Here is some more information from Udemy:

http://dna56.com/ppt

Recording With Screen Recording Software

Camtasia is excellent screen-recording software for PCs and Macs. CamStudio.com is the free version of Camtasia; it's a lot more basic. ScreenFlow is another recommended screen capturing for a Mac.

Recording with screen recording software gives you more flexibility than recording directly from PowerPoint. Also, it allows you to incorporate screen-based demonstrations (like showing a website) easily into your videos.

Technical Considerations

Udemy is pretty strict about the videos you record meeting their specifications. If they don't like the video quality, they won't approve your course and you'll have to redo your videos.

It's a good idea to do a test video first. You can get feedback on the test video directly from Udemy.

You can learn more here:

http://dna56.com/video

Recording Processes

Here is a simplified recording process if you are looking to make simple videos without investing a lot in equipment.

- o Simplified Video Production

    - Free screen recording software- http://CamStudio.org
    - Primarily screencast videos
    - Voiceover-inexpensive mike
    - Better quality mikes

    - o http://bluemic.com/snowball

    - o http://bluemic.com/yeti/

Video Formatting Setup

Videos can be formatted in a variety of ways. It's important that you make sure your video export formatting is setup correctly so it will be in the best format for Udemy.

- o Review for specifics: http://vimeo.com/help/compression
- o Screen capture: 1280 x 720
- o Export in the same size: 1280 x 720
- o Screen Capture Size = Export Size

o Make sure you are exporting your video as an MP4

Advanced Export Options

Video

Frame rate: Automatic

Key frame every: 24 frames

Quality: Smaller file size — Higher quality

Image Size: 1280 x 720 HD

☑ Preserve aspect ratio using   fit within size

Audio

☑ Encode audio

Cancel   OK

Editing

You will want to edit your videos in order to make them as professional as possible. For example, many people use placeholders, like "um...", when they are speaking, and it can be very apparent in a video.

Most PCs come with Windows Magic Movie Maker. You can use it to do some basic editing like cutting out awkward pauses or overuse of placeholders. You can also outsource your editing to a website such as Fiverr.

Resources

Here you'll find Chapter 2 resources:

- Udemy Course Content Calculations:

  http://dna56.com/calculation

- How To Use Mashup:

  http://dna56.com/mashup

- Free Teleprompters:
    - http://www.cueprompter.com/
    - http://www.easyprompter.com/

- Create A Video Recording With PowerPoint:
  http://dna56.com/ppt

- Camtasia for PC: http://camtasia.com/

- Screenflow for Mac:
  http://www.telestream.net/screenflow/overview.htm

Chapter 3: Putting Your Course Together and Extras

Supplemental Material

Now that you have your videos done, it's time to revisit your course content or outline, and add or change things before you actually upload your course to Udemy.

The reason we wanted to bring this up now before you actually get your course uploaded is because it's a hassle to have to go in and update content and change your course. One of the benefits of Udemy is you do not have to babysit your course and your content once it's already up there. The more you can think about including the things you want to include before you initially publish your course the better, because you can move on to promoting your course or whatever the next step is that you want to be doing.

The way the supplemental material is set up, it's basically the extra stuff, so it's non-video. You can have PDFs, you can have audio, you can have Excel spreadsheets, documents, PowerPoints, and it can really just be that additional type of content that you want to have in the course that helps people understand and to explain the concepts better.

If you find, when you've done some of your videos, that you have missing content or have a 'hole,' you actually can just make a whole module of written material. Every single module doesn't need to be a video. With some of your written or supplemental material, you can either include it with your course modules that are videos to help further explain your particular concept or topic in that video, A), or B), or you can have it be a standalone module by itself.

Udemy also advises that, if you're adding additional instructors on your course or additional types of content, they can also go in the supplemental materials section as well.

When you're designing a course, it's effective to have the ability to include supplemental material, because this way you can include content you want to share or cover but which doesn't necessarily lend itself well to a video or to a demonstration. By putting it in the supplemental material, it makes your course stronger and it also helps reinforce what the videos are teaching.

Branding Your Course Content

This is also a chance to brand yourself. In the supplemental material you can point to additional blogs and websites, and include resource recommendations, products and services that are related to the course.

For instance, you could perhaps have an article reinforcing the topic that you're teaching. Let's say, for example, you're doing something with gluten free and maybe you include an article about the top-ten gluten free foods to eat when you're hungry. At the bottom of that you might say, "For more gluten-free living tips, visit MyGlutenFreeBlog.com," and then they can click over to your blog on which you would have an opt-in form where they can then sign up to your email list.

Those types of content, where you're pointing people to related blogs, websites, and resources, are fine to include in supplemental material, as long as you're including related content. You're giving them content and you're pointing them to more content, which is why having a blog can be very powerful.

Udemy Terms of Service

Udemy wants to make sure that the type of content you're providing to people, whether it is in supplemental materials or in announcements, is related to what you're actually teaching or instructing. You can provide additional resources but not all-out promotion.

They're not looking for you to go, "Hey, you signed up for my free course, now buy my other products." Again, you want to point people to more free information.

Udemy has also recently updated their terms of service and they have some restriction on how many course announcements you can send and what they can include.

Make sure to review what you can and can't send.

Terms of Service- https://www.udemy.com/static/terms

Uploading Your Course

Now that you have all of your components together, it's time to upload your course to Udemy. Here are a few tips.

- Review the Udemy Course Checklist.
  http://dna56.com/course

- Print out and refer to this when you're uploading your course. The Udemy uploading a course checklist has several different segments to it. It has sections on the course itself, the promotional material, all of the information about your course, the overview, and then even the video used to market your course. Each part of your course is going to be covered under the course checklist.

- Use an outline to organize your course. It's best if you want to start with the course content itself and get that organized into sections and modules. But what you can also do is use the outline that you've previously created and you can actually use that to organize your course.

Creating Course Sections

You have a couple of different ways that you can do this. You can go ahead and section out your course from your outline. The sections themselves aren't going to be what's actually holding any content. Your section would be a chapter and then each lecture may be a sub-topic or a sub-heading underneath that chapter. The lectures will consist of your content.

You need sections. If you don't have them, they're not going to approve your course. If you have just a bunch of videos and content, you might want to think a little bit about how you can organize that into maybe four or five different sections, or something along those lines, and then you can have your content underneath each of those sections.

When you click on the add section, you enter your title and then you drag and drop it wherever you want. Then, when you're actually putting in your content, you do the same thing. You can actually label all your sections and what they call your lectures, which is actually your content. You can do all of that first before you go ahead and drop in your actual content.

Check that your sections, title and course are organized into logical sections. If you have a course on cake decorating, for example, you might have a section on types of different frostings and then basic cake decorating techniques followed by advanced techniques. So you might have three sections and then you would have your title for each.

Course Minimums

You need to have a minimum of five lectures with title description and assets. The title is the name of the lecture; the description is about what it's actually about; the asset is the actual content.

Another strategy you can do with the lectures, especially if you're making shorter videos, is make an introduction video for each of the lectures, and they actually give you the option of which videos you want to showcase, especially if it's a paid course. You can have some free videos, so that, when people are actually looking through your course and they're making their decision whether to buy or not, you can have videos for them to watch to coax them into buying or just showcase your teaching style or what you sound like, things like that, so that they get to know you before they actually buy your course.

You can choose which videos you want to give away for free. You can make none of them available for free, which is fine, too, or you could literally just make those little introductory videos for free so you're not really giving away any of the content that should definitely be paid for.

Uploading Your Content

You have a few different options for uploading your content:

- Upload one module at a time
  - o Upload supplemental material for module
  - o Write descriptions (can also be done first)

Whatever you do, you want to be organized. The method of filling in sections and lecture descriptions first makes it easy to stay organized and not miss anything. Once those are all filled in, you can then upload your content (videos, supplemental materials, etc.) for each lecture.

Adding in Your Course Information

After uploading your course content, it's time to work on a very important part of your course, your course information page. This is all the information about your course and this is really very, very important because it's about how people are going to be finding your course on Udemy and how they're going to be moving from browsers to subscribers. This is the sales page for your course.

Course Description

If you name your course the right name in terms of the keyword research right from the beginning, then you're going to be in pretty good standing for years to come and that's what we have to look at whenever we're building something. We're not just building it for today; we're building it for three years, five years, whatever it is—the long term. And we don't want somebody else who did their keyword research to get in front of us even if we put our course up before them.

That's why we have to be really smart with what we're naming our courses right from the beginning. It should be an exact keyword term, which is your main keyword, and then you have your secondary title or your subtitle, which should be another keyword term that maybe gets searched maybe a little less than or as much as the main keyword in your main title.

Obviously you're not keyword stuffing, but you are strategically naming your course so that it comes up when people are typing it in, especially when we talk about how Udemy ranks so well in Google and it's an authority site. That's one of the ways that it's going to happen for you, to get that natural, organic traffic from Google if you're naming your course correctly. That's definitely how to do it, and right now there's not a lot of competition so you can grab those keywords that get heavily searched on Google and you can own that keyword term in Udemy.

Your Sales Page

Your course description is really your sales page. The best way to put together your course description is to go on Udemy and look at a lot of different examples of course descriptions and see, especially with the courses that are popular, what people are doing to entice people to enroll in their course.

Your sales page should be powerful and persuasive. It should have an overview of your business and plenty of examples. You need to cover what the course is actually about and what it's going to be covering and why someone would want to take the course.

You also need to include your course goal and objectives, and these can be the types of things people are going to be learning from your course. What you can do is you can just review each of your lectures and say, "Okay, what did I teach there?" That's an objective; they learned how to do this.

The summary is your sales letter; the course goal and objectives are basically what people are going to get out of the big picture of your course, and the specifics that they're going to be learning. Then you also can include the intended audience.

We want to encourage you to be big and bold here when you're putting together your summary, your audience, and you're covering your objectives and so forth. You want to make it compelling and enticing and you want to make people really excited to check out the course.

You don't want to be putting barriers up; obviously you don't want to misrepresent what your course is about, but if you're offering an entry-level course where you're trying to get as much of an audience as possible, you want to paint your course with a relatively broad brush, so different types of people who are your target audience will be motivated to check out the course.

Course Description Visual Elements

There's also another really important part of your course sales letter, which is the visual element—the course graphic or video. Make sure to review their requirements on the checklist. If they don't like what you've done for the graphic, they can actually do your graphic for you; if that's one of the reasons they don't approve your course.

Create a Promo Video

If you really want to get the word out about your course, and especially if you're doing a paid course, we recommend making a video, a promotional video, because that has a lot more ability to draw people in, and with the promotional video, it can basically be the video that's free that everyone sees when they go to your course page, your landing page for your course, or you can even make it your first lecture and then it will just play for free for everybody as well.

The other thing you can do with this is, because it's your promotional video, it's an asset and you can put it on YouTube, your blog, and other social media sites, and use it to promote your course outside Udemy, too.

Here is a promo video we created for one of our courses: Promoting Your Content With Internet Radio and Podcasts

We wrote up a quick promo about the course. We got a voiceover done and then we went over to Fiverr and had somebody create a Prezi-style video, which is like an animated PowerPoint video, and then they added the voiceover to that and made a very nice promo video for us.

 On Fiverr there are a lot of people who will basically take your audio or an article and create a Prezi presentation. We would recommend maybe getting some of the upgrades to anywhere like $10-20 for your video and you can get a very nice video.

If you are struggling to decide what you want to put in your videos, remember, you don't have to make them super long; two minutes, three minutes is like a perfect video, unless you really want to get into a little bit of detail on what your course is about. Obviously that's completely up to you but, again, we're not telling you that you want to copy other people, but really study what other people are saying and what they're doing in the niche that you're involved in because that's the level that you should be living up to or even going above and beyond your competition.

It's a good strategy to browse and see what are other people doing, what kind of language are they using, what kind of videos are they using in terms of how they're trying to sell their course? And then you can either put out the same—or even better—and you'll do just fine.

If you're feeling a little overwhelmed, if it's your first course, or if it's a free course, you don't necessarily have to have a promotional video, it's just a nice tool in your arsenal to have. While we would recommend one for doing a paid course, don't let it stop you from getting your course up there.

Udemy Course Approval

When you've uploaded everything, they will usually approve your course in two to three days and they'll come back to you if there's anything that's not approved, referring to their checklist. They'll actually say, "Okay, section 3B, this needs work," or whatever. So they'll be specific and let you know and you can write them back and say, "I still don't understand what you're talking about when you said that doesn't work," and they'll give you more specifics.

Just before you submit your course, go through that checklist and make sure you've covered everything, and there shouldn't be any problems. If there is, they'll come back to you and give you the opportunity to fix them.

Resources

Here are the resources from Chapter 3:

- Blogspot
- Wordpress
- Fiverr

Chapter 4 – Free & Paid Promotion

Udemy Faculty Lounge

There are two Facebook groups that are geared toward Udemy instructors where you can share your course, get feedback and exposure, etc. So join them both because they're both really good and just shout out that you have a new course. What's great about doing that is you're connecting with other instructors and it's a great way to get your first set of reviews for your course.

You can usually connect with somebody and trade reviews. You'll find a lot of good people are just hanging out on that Facebook group and they're just looking to build traction. We would suggest doing that first before anything promotional.

You can check them out here:

https://www.facebook.com/groups/UdemyStudio/

https://www.facebook.com/groups/udemyfacultylounge/

Monetizing and Promoting Your Course

Based on our own experience with our free courses, all you really need to do is to kick start your course promotion, and get that first handful of people.

After that, if you've done your niche research and your keyword research right, as we've gone over earlier, you will start to get more and more subscribers. For example, our infographics course right now has over 4000 subscribers, believe it or not. We have done very little promotion of our own. Just thinking back to what we actually did with that particular course, I believe we announced it on Google+, to our Google+ network, and may have announced it on our Facebook page, and I think that's about it.

With a free course, you can start out with just your immediate social network and do a couple of posts. If you have a blog set up, you can do a blog post as well. You can also take your video, if you've created a promotional video for your Udemy course, and put that on YouTube and then also share that, too.

You don't necessarily want to be spending hours and hours at the beginning promoting your free course. As we were saying, if you can get those 10, 20, 30 people and you've picked and selected the right niche and the right keywords, that's going to give you that snowball effect and you're going to start to see enrollments pretty much every week or so.

You'll also see huge surges of enrollments as well over time with Udemy doing their own promotion because they run a lot of promotions where they have people just visiting the site and your course; a lot of people will see your course in these waves of traffic and then a lot of people will sign up.

General Tips

We put general tips here in this next section and we want to show you a few examples because these are free and social media and discussion-based methods to promote not only free courses but paid courses as well. These can be very effective. The problem with some of these types of tools is they can be somewhat time-consuming. You need to be thinking a little bit ahead of time about the strategy you want to have, so you're not spending an hour or two hours every day doing social media promotion because that can get kind of excessive and it can wear you down, so that's not really what you want to be doing.

Promoting courses works really well if you do have some type of content that you can actually repurpose. What's really great is that, unlike Kindle Publishing, Udemy does not have any restrictions on you repurposing or reusing your content outside of Udemy. If you have content that you've put together, or that you've taken and made slides out of or have gotten rewritten for your course, you can actually take some of that content which might be more appealing for people who haven't taken the course yet, or more for beginners or at an intro level. Then you can actually use that to help you get people onto your course.

For example, if you're doing a cake decorating course, you might have information in your course about the five popular types of frosting that people have for cake decorating. With that kind of basic level information what you can do is take that and make it into an article or into a blog post and pull it outside of Udemy and use it to help bring people back into that course again.

You can increase the reach of your article with social media by integrating it with your blog. This strategy can work really well if you not only have your social media accounts set up, you're also using some type of sharing plugin. We use a sharing plugin quite effectively in conjunction with various groups on different social media platforms.

For example, you can get a free Wordpress plugin for LinkedIn, and what's really great about this plugin is you can post to groups, so you might want to post your article to different groups with LinkedIn and that can be very powerful. LinkedIn is more for business and business networking, but let's say, for example, you have your course on social media, well, that's popular with marketers, internet marketers, business people, companies, and corporations.

You could go to LinkedIn, join a bunch of different groups that might be interested in social media and social marketing and introduce yourself in those groups, which doesn't take long. Most of them will have a little introduction thing, you can just introduce yourself. Then you can head over to your blog and you can go ahead and post a related article with maybe a coupon code for your course or a link directly to your course, and you can post it directly to all of those groups in LinkedIn on your blog. That can get you a lot of targeted traffic. I use this method all of the time.

There are some of these social media plugins that I think, in my opinion, overdo it a little bit. You don't really need 500 buttons to post everywhere. The most popular places are Twitter, Facebook, Google+, and LinkedIn and also Pinterest. If you do have accounts with sites such as StumbleUpon and Digg and all those other social sites, that would be good, but, if you can, stick to the basic five to share your content with.

Strategically, using these sharing buttons is very powerful. The other one we want to draw your attention to quickly is Google+. Google+ allows you to share your blog post with a plugin to everybody you're connected with on Google+, but another thing with Google+ is that it also has communities, like LinkedIn groups and Facebook groups.

You just have to be careful, though, that you don't over-share and post your thing in 20 different groups at once on Google+ because they can get a little weird about that. But groups and community sharing can be really powerful for getting the word out about your Udemy course. It can be very effective because you're really tapping into those targeted audiences.

Another great set of tools is what I like to call social curation, or community tools. These are basically, again, sites where you can add content and then it's shared with other people who belong to that community, and it's almost like curating content, where you can share not only your content, but other people's content as well.

Two examples are list.ly and Scoop.it, those are both newer, popular sites where people have had success promoting their Udemy courses.

Then of course there are also the different groups and communities we've just mentioned with Google, Facebook, LinkedIn and even Yahoo.

You can also use answer sites, like Yahoo Answers, and some of the other answer sites where people might be having a question on your topic, and you can go and answer that question and you can even have some information or link back to your blog with some more information.

Google Alerts

You could try this particular strategy: open up a Google alert at http://Google.com/alerts, put in your keywords, and then Google will send you all the indexed links where your keywords show up. That can be a really powerful strategy for finding out what people are talking about and then you can go in and drop in your information or engage with those people.

List.ly

List.ly is a popular site where you can make and share lists. You can also put this on your site as well with a widget. A lot of Udemy instructors like to use list.ly because they can include their course, they can include other types of information as well. List.ly is a great tool for just making sure you're getting the word out and promoting your course, whether it's free or whether it's paid.

Scoop.it.

Another cool tool is called Scoop.it. Scoop.it allows you to share information and then you can scoop it and put it into your own curation. It also has the integrative social media buttons and it has comments as well.

Udemy also has sharing buttons. If you go to your course listing page just as a visitor, or you look at other courses, you'll see that they have all these social sharing buttons on each page as well.

Another tool we want to highlight is slide and doc sharing sites like SlideShare, and Scribd. The reason we're mentioning slide sharing sites is because, once you already have all these PowerPoint slides that you've put together for your Udemy course, you can take some of the slides and make some mini PowerPoint courses and put those up on the slide sharing sites with a link back to your course.

Again, you're repurposing content, you're not having to reinvent the wheel. Also, that type of thing is very easy to have somebody set that up for you, for example on Fiverr, where you can have someone post to the different sites for you. You can even have them create a PowerPoint from an outline or repurpose the PowerPoint you already have and then they can go ahead and post those to the different sites.

Monetizing Your Free Course

Make sure you include resources and recommendations in your supplemental materials that ideally link back to your blog. That is something that you do need to have really set up ahead of time because, if you do change or add anything to your course, your course has to go through the approval process again.

TIP: If you are promoting affiliate programs on your blog, or through an email list you have setup on your blog, make sure you include an affiliate disclosure that states you receive an affiliate commission if they make a sale through your link.

Course Announcements

The other thing that you can do is send out course announcements and these can be things where you're providing more information about the topic, more education, more related content. Basically, what you can do with this is lead those people back to your blog where you might have a blog post or you might have some more information that they can download or take a look at.

Udemy, though, has really cracked down on course announcements. You cannot promote other courses with your affiliate link any longer through course announcements.

You can read some of their new guidelines here and proceed accordingly:

http://dna56.com/guideline

Paid Course Promotion

Surveys

Let's talk about going from free to paid courses. If you would like to create a paid course after a free course, a course survey can be a great tool. You can even have it as part of the course, like a supplementary thing or like a module, and then take that information and go and create that paid course with it as well.

Surveys are great because, a lot of times when you're creating your free course, it's going to be just kind of basic information or general information, but who knows? Your course subscribers may be interested in something that you're not covering that thoroughly in the free course and they want that content and that can be your next step, creating that content and then selling it.

Here are some free survey tools:

- Survey Monkey (https://www.surveymonkey.com/)
- Google Docs (not as fancy, but it's free) (https://doc.google.com/)
- SurveyGizmo (has a free trial) (http://www.surveygizmo.com/)
- eSurveysPro (http://www.esurveyspro.com/ (if you click on pricing and go to the bottom, there is a free plan)

You give your free course subscribers a survey and use their responses to shape your paid course. Basically you're asking them, "What do you want me to teach you?" or "What do you still want to learn after you've done the free course?" Then you can take that information and go and construct your paid course with it. This is a very powerful strategy.

What you would do then, of course, is get a set amount of free subscribers, perhaps 300-500, with some of the promotional methods that we've been discussing and keep in touch with them, maybe send them some other freebies through the course announcements, keep engagement with them. Then, when your course is ready, you offer them the promotion; you create that promotional code with the coupon link and offer them a special discount to your paid course.

Udemy allows you to send two promotional announcements a month to your current course subscribers, so you can certainly notify them about your new course.

You can really stress that the reason they're getting such a good deal is because they're your free course subscribers and you want them to be the first people to check out your paid course.

Course Coupons

Here is some info on creating course coupons:

http://dna56.com/coupon

Of course, you can promote your course via coupons outside Udemy as well. For example, it's really important to get those initial reviews, and you can do that by generously handing out free course coupons to people, particularly other Udemy instructors.

You can also ask friends or colleagues in your field to leave you a review; you can get some of those initial reviews by having them check out your free course.

Ask people to leave you an honest review, you don't want to pressure them into leaving you the five stars.

We've been talking a lot about promotional coupons and one of the things we want to stress is that most instructors are driving most of the traffic to their courses from promotional coupons. It's a two-tier thing, where the prices you see when you go to Udemy and you surf around and you look at all those classes, aren't, in a sense, the real prices. Those are just the full prices that are on there.

Most instructors are driving most of their traffic to those courses through a discounted price. That's really something you want to be thinking about with your own pricing, as you don't want to under-price your course because you're going to be offering it to people at a discount, and you want to make sure that you're getting a fair price if you're offering a discounted rate on the course.

Advertising

As with promoting any type of product, you just need to get a little bit creative, but keep in mind that, with paid courses, if you do want to ramp up your income quickly, it might be good to be considering a little bit of an advertising budget, unless you want to go with the method of moving your free people over to paid people, which you can always do as well. But if you want to just start off with doing paid courses and you want to drive a lot of traffic to them, you want to be thinking a bit about some methods of capturing some paid traffic.

The majority of people on Udemy who are driving a lot of traffic to their courses are using pay per click; a lot of them use Google Adwords; a lot of them use Facebook ads.

You can also do a lot of other things as well. We've talked a little bit about blog marketing and social media platforms. If you do have a list, you can even just promote your course to your list. We've been seeing several other marketers do that as well where they have a very large list of people, email subscribers, and then they go ahead and promote their paid Udemy courses to that list.

Corporations, Businesses and Group Buys

Now, this is another really powerful strategy that we're going to share with you here, that there are a lot of corporations out there, businesses and groups, who buy courses for their employees.

You can actually contact these businesses and organizations and, again, you can hire somebody to do this for you; you can hire telemarketers and people like that or you can do direct mail or you can even use email. You can offer them a specialized promotional code for their employees and you can get their employees to enroll as a group, as a group buy.

I know that this is also a very powerful strategy and there are a number of Udemy instructors who have been using this. You can even do this as an affiliate for other courses!

Now of course it would depend on the type of course you're offering and so forth, but this can be very powerful. Imagine talking to a company that has 4,000 employees and they get 500 to 1,000 of those people to enroll onto your course. That's very powerful.

In fact, Udemy is actually starting to work with corporations and organizations directly and they actually have a program called Udemy for Organizations.

https://www.udemy.com/organizations/

As an organization, you can create a training library under your name so when your employees log on, let's say it's General Electric or something, they log on and see General

Electric on the dashboard, but they're actually watching a Udemy course. Organizations, at least for right now, sign up for free and get on the list for this, where they can have their own branded Udemy course inside their organization.

If you think about it, there are hundreds of thousands of corporations out there that all need specific skills. Those organizations don't have the time to teach and train and put together a course for them. But if they could have one where it looked very seamless with the other training that they have for their business, and people could just get on and not be taken out of their company website presence, many would sign up.

We're predicting that this approach is going to become bigger and bigger and it's definitely something that we wanted to share with you because that way you can be more aware of that as a rising trend in terms of getting your course out there.

Once you have got to a point where you feel like you're getting some core subscribers regularly or you have all engines firing, you really want to be thinking about planning your next course. This can be very powerful. If you have one niche you want to explore with a variety of courses or if you have some related niches you want to explore, you can really take this in a wide variety of directions, but you do want to be thinking about how each of those courses can help support what you're doing outside of Udemy—building your list, making affiliate income for you, making paid course income for you. With a little bit of planning and forethought with this, you can actually then make sure your next course is strategic and you're planning your next course strategically.

That's really what it's all about. It's about finishing a course, promoting it, monetizing, planning your next course and then rinsing and repeating, doing so in a strategic way so each course is building on the previous one and it just becomes easier and easier to get those course subscribers and to get those people on your list and to get the affiliate income and to get the paid course income.

Resources

Here are resources for Chapter 4:

- List.ly: http://list.ly/
- Scoop.it: http://www.scoop.it/
- Slideshare: http://www.slideshare.net/
- Doctoc: http://www.docstoc.com/
- Scribd: http://www.scribd.com/
- Instructor Dos & Don'ts : http://dna56.com/guideline
- Survey Monkey: https://www.surveymonkey.com/
- Google Docs: https://doc.google.com/

- SurveyGizmo: http://www.surveygizmo.com/
- eSurveysPro: http://www.esurveyspro.com/

Conclusion

You really have all you need right now to create, publish, sell and promote a Udemy course! Even if you are creating a course to give away for free, it's a great strategy because you can put resources in your course for people to check out which will bring them to even more of your web properties that you own online (like your blog, website, YouTube channel, social media, etc.). Do you see how everything now works together for a complete marketing funnel? It's a beautiful thing!

Remember what we said at the very beginning of this book about doing the work once and having it work over and over again for you?

Here is a reminder: We believe and live by this rule: have the content that you create ONCE work for you over and over again in many different ways.

The same holds true with any content you create for a Udemy course. You can always use any part of the content of your course for anything else you are giving away or selling online.

For instance, if you create a video for the Udemy course, you can then take that video and offer it as a free gift somewhere else. There is no piece of content that you create that you can't keep using over and over again for more ways to promote, reach more people and sell online!

We wish you the best of luck with Udemy. We think this is a very smart way of marketing and reaching an entirely new group of people who are looking for information online. Take advantage of that. Take action. Whatever you create will always be an asset to you and your business.

To Your Success,

Deb & Amy

http://amydebcreations.com

Your Feedback

Thank you for taking the time to read our book. Please kindly leave your feedback on Amazon here:

http://dna56.com/udemy-review

We would love to hear from you!

www.ingramcontent.com/pod-product-compliance
Lightning Source LLC
Chambersburg PA
CBHW071757170526
45167CB00003B/1064